DUNDER QUIZLIN

OTHER BOOKS BY ALEX MITCHELL

Quizzin' Nine-Nine: A Brooklyn Nine-Nine Quiz Book
Parks & Interrogation: A Parks & Recreation Quiz Book
Q & AC-12: A Line of Duty Quiz Book
Know Your Schitt: A Schitt's Creek Quiz Book
Examilton: A Hamilton Quiz Book
Stranger Thinks: A Stranger Things Quiz Book
The El Clued Brothers: A Peep Show Quiz Book

Dunder Quizlin

The Office (US) Quiz Book

Published by Beartown Press

Copyright © 2020 Alex Mitchell

ISBN: 9798690751449

This book is unofficial, unauthorized and in no way associated with the Office television production in any of its magnificent forms. Please don't set Dwight on me.

"You only live once? False. You live every day. You only die once."

Dwight K. Schrute

Contents

Introduction	11
Season One	13
Michael	15
That's What She Said	17
Dwight	19
Season Two	21
Jim	22
Anagrams	23
Pam	24
Season Three	25
Pranks	27
Toby	29
Andy	30
Season Four	31
Diseases	33
Phyllis	34
The Accounting Department	35
Season Five	36
Dwight's Perfect Crime	38
Kelly & Ryan	39
Season Six	41
Stanley	43
Who Said It?	44
Season Seven	46
Complete the Quote	48
Cast & Crew	50

Season Eight	51
The Hardcore Nerd Round	52
The UK Version	53
Season Nine	54
Tiebreakers	55
ANSWERS	58

Introduction

The American version of *The Office* is perhaps one of the most beloved, most quotable and most rewatchable sitcoms of all-time. Even now, after having watched every episode multiple times, it's still my go-to show.

It's also why it's the perfect subject for a quiz book. Here's what you have on your hands:

- Over 400 quiz questions about The Office.

- The questions are separated into 30 themed rounds, plus an extra set of tiebreakers to separate the Wonder Dunders from the Snifflin' Mifflins.

- Answer sheets for each round are located in the second half of the book.

- If you haven't seen all of *The Office*, please be aware that this book contains spoilers (obviously).

So, if you're ready to prove who's top of the Scotts and make your play for a Dundie, let's get started...

Season One

1. In the pilot episode, how long does Michael tell us he's worked for Dunder Mifflin?
2. What does Michael say he calls Jan Levinson-Gould (though not because he's afraid of her)?
3. What does Jim (correctly) day is Pam's favorite yoghurt flavor?
4. When pranking Pam, what does Michael accuse her of stealing from the office?
5. Which item belonging to Dwight does Jim encase in Jell-O?
6. What is the name of the representative who arrives to lead Diversity Day at the office?
7. What does Michael have written on the card on his head during the diversity game?
8. Which colleague needs medical coverage for dermatitis?
9. With which phrase does Pam say Jim instructed her to respond if Dwight ever asks her if she wants to be involved in something secret?
10. What donation per mile does Michael pledge to Oscar's nephew's charity walkathon (before he actually realizes the donation is per mile)?
11. Whose birthday is celebrated, despite it being a month away?

12. Who does Michael pick for his basketball team's "secret weapon"?

13. In that basketball game, what was the losing team's forfeit going to be?

14. What is the name of the saleswoman who visits the office in the season finale?

15. What product is she selling?

Answers on page 59

Michael

1. What statement is printed on Michael's coffee mug, which he purchased for himself?
2. Complete the lineup of Michael's heroes: Bob Hope, Abraham Lincoln, Bono and who?
3. How did Michael lose his college tuition money?
4. What is Michael's middle name?
5. At what age did Michael learn to talk?
6. What proportion of his heritage does Michael claim to be Native American?
7. In his *Fundle Bundle* appearance, how many kids did Michael say that he wanted to have?
8. What was Michael cooking on his George Foreman Grill before he burned his foot?
9. Which basketball team does Michael support?
10. What is the name of the separate paper company Michael sets up in season five?
11. How many minutes did Michael work at Dunder Mifflin, as calculated by his colleagues in his farewell song?
12. What is Michael's nickname in the warehouse?
13. According to Michael, he once went how many years without having sex?
14. Which Dundie does Michael almost always award to Ryan?

15. Which beloved item of clothing does Michael always get dry-cleaned?

Answers on page 60

That's What She Said

Can you complete these "That's what she said" setups?

1. "Dip it in the water so it'll slide down your _____ more easily." - Michael.
2. "It was easy to get in but impossible to _____ up." - Holly.
3. "You should put _____ on it." - Oscar.
4. "Well, you always left me satisfied and _____..." - Jim.
5. "And up comes the _____." - Michael.
6. "Dwight, get out of my _____!" - Kelly.
7. "Oscar, would you reach over and touch his _____?" - Michael.
8. "I can't force you to go down, but I can _____ you." - Michael.
9. "The trick is to do it face down with the _____ in your mouth." - Dwight.
10. "Oscar is my _____. That's easy, gimme a hard one." - Michael.
11. "Comedy is a place where the mind goes to _____ itself." - David Brent.
12. "It _____ when you bang it." - Michael.
13. "Michael, I can't believe you _____." - Dwight.

14. "There's no way you guys are making this _____ with just your mouths." - Clark.

15. "This is going to feel so good, getting this thing off my _____." - Michael.

Answers on page 61

Dwight

1. What is Dwight's middle name?
2. Which two animals does Dwight assess that his level of pace lies somewhere between?
3. Dwight's perfect crime involves stealing what?
4. In Dwight's fantasy job (in which he co-owns a Bed & Breakfast with Satan), conjured up while attempting to torment Jim, what is his annual salary?
5. What is Dwight's all-time favorite movie?
6. Dwight never took a sick day at Dunder Mifflin, even when he had which illness?
7. Which band did Dwight invite Clark to see with him?
8. What medical procedure did Dwight apparently perform on himself growing up?
9. What name did Dwight give to the gym he opened within the Dunder Mifflin office building?
10. What is the name of Dwight's cousin, who is also Hay King of the Schrutes?
11. Who is the only person Dwight says he tips?
12. What is Dwight's favorite cereal?
13. How many rules does Dwight say that Schrute boys must learn before the age of five?
14. What is the main produce grown on the farm owned by Dwight and the Schrute family?

15. For which sleight was Dwight shunned by his family from the age of four until his sixth birthday?

Answers on page 62

Season Two

1. Which award does Pam win at the Dundies?
2. What is the full name of the office sporting event created by Jim and Pam?
3. Who started the fire?
4. Who does Michael fire on Halloween?
5. To which venue does Michael switch his and Jan's meeting with big potential client Christian?
6. What does Michael buy for Ryan in Secret Santa?
7. What is the name of the ship captain on the *Princess*?
8. What is Oscar actually doing on his sick day?
9. Who leaves the disgusting "thing" on the carpet in Michael's office?
10. Whose desk does Michael take while his carpet is being replaced?
11. What does Roy gift to Pam for Valentine's Day?
12. What company-wide award does Dwight win?
13. What is Michael's (unfortunate) online dating name?
14. At whose concert did Michael smoke a "clove cigarette", leading him to be concerned about Dwight's urine testing?
15. As a result of a prank by Jim, what does Dwight's security badge show his middle name as?

Answers on page 63

Jim

1. What is the sea-themed nickname given to Jim by Andy?
2. What is Jim's middle name?
3. Where does Jim plan to be while Pam is marrying Roy?
4. What are the names of Jim's two brothers?
5. Which city's sports teams does Jim support?
6. Where does Jim propose to Pam?
7. How long after they started dating did he buy the engagement ring?
8. What is the name of the sports marketing company which Jim co-creates?
9. What is the name of Jim's eldest daughter?
10. What did Jim get for Pam when he was her Secret Santa?
11. Using Dwight's stationary, Jim sent faxes to Dwight claiming to be who?
12. Which sound does Jim train Dwight to expect an Altoid with?
13. Who does Jim describe to Dwight as "a crime-fighting beaver"?
14. To which city do Jim and Pam move in the series finale?
15. What is Jim's position in that company at the end of *The Office*?

Answers on page 64

Anagrams

Can you unscramble these fiendish acronyms to reveal the names of The Office characters and other elements of the show?

1. Horny Award?
2. Battered Corn?
3. A Laborer Friction?
4. Sitcom Chalet?
5. Old Unloving Jeans?
6. Blind Lip Harry?
7. Maybe Slep?
8. A Cavilled Wad?
9. Twitched Shrug?
10. Hamper Jilt?
11. Wise Bagel?
12. Lake Look Pry?
13. A Nerdy Brand?
14. Ennobled Frosty?
15. Annoys Hustled?

Answers on page 65

Pam

1. How long had Pam been engaged to Roy at the very start of *The Office*?
2. What is Pam's middle name?
3. From which restaurant chain is Pam banned?
4. What game does Pam usually play on her computer at work?
5. What sport did Pam attend a camp for most summers?
6. What song does Pam sing at the office's funeral for a dead bird?
7. What is Pam's job at the Michael Scott Paper Company?
8. What is the name of Pam's son?
9. Where did Pam say goodbye to Michael, as he left the company to be with Holly?
10. What does Pam use to make the medals for the office Olympics?
11. What does Pam study at the Pratt Institute?
12. What was the name of the comic Pam made for Jim one Christmas?
13. While she was in New York, who did Pam dress up as for Halloween?
14. What is Pam's mother's name?
15. Where do Pam and Jim get married?

Answers on page 66

Season Three

1. Which other Dunder Mifflin branch is merged with Scranton?
2. Who is mistaken for a hooker at the Philadelphia convention?
3. What video game does Jim's new team play at work (at which he's not very good)?
4. How long is Dwight forced to do Michael's laundry for, after his attempted coup?
5. What is the name of Michael's farmer boss and mentor, whose death is mourned with an unorthodox grief session?
6. Which free food item do Michael and Stanley spend most of a workday waiting in line for?
7. Who does Michael propose to on their ninth date?
8. What is Andy's three-part strategy to make himself the "number 2 man in Scranton within six weeks"?
9. While attempting to make a stand against stereotyping and racism, who does Michael say that he trusts more than Jesus?
10. Where do Andy and Michael meet their Christmas party dates?

11. Apart from Dwight (whose attempt surely cannot be considered a success), which character successfully walked across the hot coals?

12. Where does Dwight get a job after briefly leaving Dunder Mifflin?

13. What creature does Dwight discover in the ceiling, later catching it with a garbage bag over Meredith's head?

14. When Roy and his brother Kenny smash up the bar in the aftermath of his breakup with Pam, where does the money used to pay off the bar owner apparently come from?

15. Whose vehicle does the watermelon smash on after being bounced off the trampoline in the car park by Michael?

Answers on page 67

Pranks

1. From which item does Jim construct a "desk fence" to separate Dwight's area from his?
2. Who did Pam convince Dwight to race around the building, even though the other person wasn't actually competing, and she was "timing" him with a thermometer?
3. Karen programmed the '9' button on Jim's phone to speed-dial a telephone number located where?
4. In season two, Jim gave Dwight some debatable public-speaking tips borrowed from which politician?
5. How much did Jim's Dwight costume cost?
6. Jim sets up a macro on Dwight's computer so that every time Dwight types his own name, it is changed to which word?
7. In reality, what was the "gaydar device" Jim sent to Dwight, which Dwight is startled to discover beeps while pointing it at himself?
8. Instead of a stripper, Jim hires an impersonator of which historical figure for Pam's bachelorette party?
9. What did Jim wear to mock Dwight's office dress code, which backfired somewhat when Charles Miner from Corporate attended the officer on the same day?

10. Which language do Jim and Pam take a class in so that they can trick Dwight into thinking there is a bomb in the office?

11. Dwight pays Erin to announce in the office that she had won what type of contest?

12. Under what pen name does Jim author *The Ultimate Guide to Throwing a Garden Party*, to derail Dwight's event at Schrute Farms?

13. What does Dwight use Jim's credit card details to buy as an undetectable prank when their Christmas bonuses are at stake?

14. In season eight, Dwight and Stanley collude to convince an unknowing Jim to provide them with vast amounts of which foodstuff as part of an ongoing prank?

15. What is the name of the Halperts' actor friend, who pretends to be Jim while Jim is at the dentist (including replacing him in the family photos on Jim's desk)?

Answers on page 68

Toby

1. What is Toby's daughter's name?
2. What is Toby's job title at Dunder Mifflin?
3. What type of stuffed animal does Toby spend the evening trying to win from a claw machine for Pam?
4. Which country does Toby move to at the end of season four?
5. A broken neck forces Toby to curtail his travels and return to Dunder Mifflin, but how did he injure himself?
6. A clash with which event means Toby is forced to decline the invitation to Pam's art show?
7. What item did Michael give Toby as a gift before he moved to Costa Rica?
8. And what did the heart-warming message on that gift say?
9. What does Michael give to Toby instead?
10. At which game did Toby beat Michael at the casino?
11. What genre of novel does Toby write?
12. For which case did Toby serve jury duty?
13. What subject does Toby have a Masters in?
14. Which of his colleagues dressed up as Toby for Halloween?
15. What food is Toby allergic to?

Answers on page 69

Andy

1. Which college did Andy attend (and later work at)?
2. What is the name of Andy's a cappella group?
3. What is Andy's middle name?
4. Which part of Andy's body is extremely sensitive?
5. On Jim's "advice", what song does Andy play on the banjo (and sing in falsetto) for Pam?
6. What musical did Andy star in a local production of?
7. Where does Andy sail the family boat to?
8. What does Andy do after Jim and Pam hide his phone in the ceiling of the office?
9. What does Andy do to David Wallace's car in order to get fired and burn his Dunder Mifflin bridges?
10. With which song does Andy serenade his colleagues goodbye?
11. Where is Andy's 'Nard Dog' tattoo located?
12. Which reality TV show does Andy audition for?
13. What nickname does he attract after his emotional appearance on that show goes viral?
14. Which political figure does Nellie convince Andy he is related to?
15. What is Andy's job at the end of *The Office*?

Answers on page 70

Season Four

1. Who wins the fun run?
2. Who does Michael accidentally hit with his car?
3. Angela gets mad when Dwight euthanizes one of her cats. What was its name?
4. Who wins the selling challenge: Dwight or the new company website?
5. What are the themes of the three themed rooms in Schrute Farms bed and breakfast?
6. While staying there Jim and Pam get Dwight to read them and excerpt from which book?
7. Michael gets a second job, working nights to service the debts Jan's heavy spending is putting them into. What is the job?
8. What is the name of Dwight's *Second Life* character?
9. And what is the name of Jim's character in the same game?
10. Which two items does Michael demand to prove that he is capable of surviving in the wilderness?
11. With which song do Michael and Dwight serenade the grave of the chair model (seemingly for hours)?
12. Later in the season, Ryan launches "Dunder Mifflin Infinity 2.0", but why was the first website he launched shut down?

13. Who buys Andy's car?

14. What is the only item Michael has taken to promote Dunder Mifflin's stand at the summer internship fair?

15. Toby prepares to leave in the season finale, but what is the name of his replacement?

Answers on page 71

Diseases

Can you pick the diseases that were really submitted to Dwight during the health plan selection, from the ones we've made up?

1. Mad Cow Disease?
2. Spontaneous Dental Hydroplosion?
3. Executive Bloating?
4. Severe Hangover?
5. General Illness?
6. Flesh-Eating Bacteria?
7. Hot Dog Fingers?
8. Anal Fissures?
9. Missing Nipple?
10. Government Created Killer Nanorobot Infection?
11. Nakatomi Syndrome?
12. Inverted Penis?
13. Count Choculitis?
14. Belgian Arthritis?
15. Excessively Small Thumbs?

Answers on page 72

Phyllis

1. With which fellow Dunder Mifflin employee did Phyllis attend high school?
2. Who does Phyllis take to a beauty parlor for a gaudy makeover in preparation for a sales call?
3. What is Phyllis' maiden name?
4. What is the name of Phyllis' husband?
5. Which award does Phyllis win at the first Dundies?
6. What was Phyllis' nickname in high school?
7. How much does Phyllis' hug sell for at the auction?
8. Which theme does Phyllis choose for her first office Christmas party as head of the party-planning committee?
9. Who fixes Phyllis back after she injures it dancing at Michael's "Café Disco"?
10. Who accidentally wore the same outfit as Phyllis on Casual Friday?
11. Why did Phyllis include Michael in her wedding party?
12. Who catches Phyllis' bouquet at her wedding?
13. Who does Phyllis dress as for the Halloween costume contest in season seven?
14. What does Phyllis knit for Michael as a leaving present?
15. At what age does Phyllis say she had her first orgasm?

Answers on page 73

The Accounting Department

1. What is Kevin's surname?
2. Who do both Angela and Oscar enter a romantic relationship with?
3. What is Kevin's Police cover band called?
4. How many "procreation attempts" does Angela negotiate with Dwight?
5. Aside from having sex with men, what does Oscar claim is "the gayest thing about [him]"?
6. What does Kevin claim is "the thing I probably do best"?
7. What number does Kevin invent to fix his accounting errors?
8. What TV show do his colleagues erroneously believe Oscar loves?
9. What does Toby get Angela for Secret Santa?
10. What does Oscar want to buy with the surplus budget?
11. What career move does Oscar make at the end of *The Office*?
12. What is the name of Angela's son?
13. Who is Angela's son's godfather?
14. What was Kevin's nickname in high school?
15. What is Dwight's pet name for Angela?

Answers on page 74

Season Five

1. What does Kelly buy from Creed in an attempt to lose weight?
2. What is Andy's nickname within his a cappella group?
3. Which song do Michael and Holly perform to open the internal seminar about business ethics?
4. Jan comes into the office for her baby shower, accompanied by her already-born baby - but what has Jan named her?
5. Michael comes up with the "clever" acronym C.R.I.M.E A.I.D after the office is broken into (due to him and Holly leaving the door unlocked after a romantic interlude on the stairs), but what does the acronym stand for?
6. Which character do Dwight, Creed and Kevin all dress up as for Halloween?
7. David Wallace gets Holly transferred back to which Dunder Mifflin branch?
8. Where do Andy and Angela arrange to hold their wedding?
9. Michael attempts to plant what he believes is marijuana in Toby's desk. What is actually in the bag?
10. What does the office agree to do with the surplus budget?

11. Which doll does Dwight purchase in bulk, identifying it as the most popular toy that Christmas and selling it to desperate parents for a profit?

12. Which actress do the office debate the hotness of for an episode?

13. Which two employees does Charles install as temporary receptionist and "productivity tzar"?

14. What does Dwight use as invisible ink when organizing his clandestine meeting in the warehouse?

15. What does Dwight ask the rest of the office for in order to fix Phyllis's back?

Answers on page 75

Dwight's Perfect Crime

Can you fill in the blanks in Dwight's self-described "perfect crime"?

"What is my perfect crime? I break into (1)_____ at midnight. Do I go for the vault? No, I go for the (2)_____. It's priceless. As I'm taking it down, a woman catches me. She tells me to stop. It's her father's business. She's (3)_____. I say no. We make love all night. In the morning, the cops come and I escape in one of their (4)_____. I tell her to meet me in (5)_____, but I go to (6)_____. I don't trust her. Besides, I like the (7)_____. (8)_____ years later, I get a postcard. I have a son and he's the (9)_____ _____. This is where the story gets interesting. I tell [answer to 3] to meet me in (10)_____ by the (11)_____. She's been waiting for me all these years. She's never taken another lover. I don't care. I don't show up. I go to (12)_____. That's where I stashed the [answer to 2]."

Answers on page 76

Kelly & Ryan

1. What is Kelly's surname?
2. What does Jim give to Kelly for Secret Santa?
3. What is the name of the series for which Ryan takes nude photographs of Kelly?
4. Ryan holds an MBA from which school?
5. Which celebrity does Erin tell Kelly that she looks like?
6. After he gets promoted to corporate, what is the name of the initiative Ryan introduces to revolutionize the company with new technology?
7. Which Dunder Mifflin colleague does Kelly date during seasons four and five in an attempt to make Ryan jealous?
8. Which offence is Ryan arrested for in the season four finale?
9. In season five, Kelly manipulates Jim and Dwight's customer survey scores after they neglect to attend her wrap party for which TV show?
10. Where is Ryan working when Michael convinces him to join the Michael Scott Paper Company?
11. What is the name of the social networking platform Ryan devises?
12. In season eight, Pam sets Kelly up with her children's pediatrician. What is his name?

13. Which state do Kelly and Ryan move to (for unrelated reasons) at the start of season nine?

14. What is the name of Ryan's son?
15. What food is he allergic to (which Ryan gives him to cause a diversion to talk to Kelly at Dwight and Angela's wedding)?

Answers on page 77

Season Six

1. What sport does Michael claim he "should've known doesn't exist" as a kid?
2. Who becomes co-manager of the branch with Michael?
3. At Jim and Pam's wedding which song do the guests from the office perform to in the aisle?
4. Who accidentally reveals Pam's pregnancy at the rehearsal dinner?
5. Pam accidentally tears her veil before the wedding, but how does Jim equalize this on his own outfit?
6. Where do Jim and Pam go on their honeymoon?
7. Who accidentally cancels Jim's credit card?
8. Which variety of fish occupies the pond into which Michael falls?
9. What is the name of the murder mystery game Michael plays in the office to distract the staff from Dunder Mifflin's financial troubles?
10. Who is controversially selected as employee of the month?
11. What Secret Santa present does Michael give to Dwight, having the parts delivered to him separately over a series of weeks?
12. What is David Wallace's proposed business venture after he leaves Dunder Mifflin?

13. Over footage of which children's television character does Oscar dub Kevin's voice?

14. Who is accepted onto the Sabre minority executive training program "Print in All Colors"?

15. Who buys Scranton Business Park?

Answers on page 78

Stanley

1. What is Stanley's ex-wife named?
2. What is the name of Stanley's mistress, who was his nurse during physiotherapy?
3. How does Stanley take his iced tea?
4. What puzzle is Stanley typically seen doing?
5. What does Stanley give to Phyllis when he returns from retirement?
6. What is the name of Stanley's daughter?
7. What is Stanley's catchphrase, established in season eight?
8. What award does Stanley win at the first Dundies?
9. How many pounds does Stanley shed in the weight loss competition?
10. What wedding gift does Stanley give to Pam and Jim, originally intended as a wedding gift for Pam and Roy?
11. What is Stanley's role in *Threat Level Midnight*?
12. Which other Dunder Mifflin branch does Stanley come close to joining?
13. What is Stanley's favorite day of the year?
14. What incident at the office ultimately causes Stanley to have a heart attack?
15. Who does Stanley sit across from in the office?

Answers on page 79

Who Said It?

Can you remember which characters delivered these classic lines?

1. "I talk a lot, so I've learned to tune myself out."
2. "If I don't have some cake soon, I might die."
3. "Sometimes I'll start a sentence and I don't even know where it's going. I just hope I find it along the way."
4. "I got six numbers. One more, would've been a complete telephone number."
5. "I wish there was a way to know you're in the good old days before you've actually left them."
6. "We have a gym at home. It's called the bedroom."
7. "I don't want to be married in a tent like a hobo."
8. "Whenever I'm about to do something, I think, 'Would an idiot do that?' and if they would, I do not do that thing."
9. "I have six roommates, which are better than friends because they have to give you one month's notice before they leave."
10. "So, the guy shows me the deck he's built. And I'm like, I'll call this a deck if it'll make you happy, but this is just a porch without a roof."
11. "Everything I have I owe to this job...this stupid, wonderful, boring, amazing job."

12. "What has two thumbs and likes to bone your mom? This guy!"

13. "Me think, why waste time say lot word, when few word do trick?"

14. "Like my mom always says: talk classy, act nasty."

15. "There's a lot of beauty in ordinary things. Isn't that kind of the point?"

Answers on page 80

Season Seven

1. What is the name of Michael's nephew, who joins the branch as an assistant in the season opener?
2. Which shopping complex does Dwight encourage the team to boycott after he was refused service?
3. Why does Michael arrive for work wearing a false moustache?
4. Which trio do Jim, Pam and Cece dress as for Halloween?
5. After a mishap involving her new dress and a dirty nappy, Cece is christened wearing a t-shirt of which band?
6. Erin and Gabe invite the office to Gabe's for a viewing party for which show?
7. Which organization buys WUHPF.com from Ryan?
8. According to Dwight, what is the greatest snowball?
9. In *Threat Level Midnight*, who plays the President of the United States?
10. What does Michael spend on an engagement ring for Holly?
11. What award does DeAngelo win at the Dundies?
12. Which film does Pam spend most of the day watching while Michael is saying his final goodbyes?
13. To which state do Michael and Holly move?
14. To which song does DeAngelo perform the feat of juggling invisible balls for the office?

15. What is DeAngelo trying to do when he suffers the injury that ultimately puts him in a coma? Slam-dunking a basketball.

Answers on page 81

Complete the Quote

Fill in the blanks to complete these quotes from *The Office*.

1. "Would I rather be feared or loved? Easy. Both. I want people to be _____ _____ _____ _____ _____ _____ _____." - Michael.
2. "My _____ shoes were a huge conversation piece. But man, my dogs are barking!" - Kevin.
3. "_____ are the peacocks of the business world; all show, no meat." - Dwight.
4. "How is it possible that in five years, I've had two engagements and only one _____?" - Pam.
5. "I... DECLARE... _____!" - Michael.
6. "I'm not superstitious, but I am _____ _____ _____." - Michael.
7. "A strongman crushed a turtle. I laughed and I cried. Not bad for a day in the life of a _____ _____ company." - Creed.
8. "You know what would be the hottest thing ever? A pregnant _____ _____." - Toby.
9. "I love the smell of _____ on a woman." - Kevin.
10. "The worst thing about prison was the _____." - Michael/Prison Mike.

11. "Just so you know. You and me, I don't think that's ridiculous. _____ _____ _____, _____ _____." - Darryl.

12. "I'm in love! I was hit by Cupid's _____!" - Michael.

13. "Oh, so, Dwight gave me this wooden mallard as a gift. I found a recording device in it. Yes. So. I think if I play it just right, I can get Dwight to live out the plot of _____ _____." - Jim.

14. "Welcome to the Hotel Hell. Check-in time in now, check-out time is never. [...] And the sheets are made of _____!" - Dwight.

15. "So, one afternoon, while walking home from school, quirky 10th grader Becky Walters finds a wounded Pegasus in the woods. And she becomes... The _____ _____." - Pam.

Answers on page 82

Cast & Crew

How well do you know the cast and crew of *The Office*?

1. Which British duo created the original version of *The Office*, and executive-produced the US version?
2. Who developed the American version of The Office, and served as its showrunner for the first four seasons?
3. Who plays Michael Scott?
4. Who plays Dwight Schrute?
5. Who directed the most episodes of *The Office*?
6. Who plays Pam Beesly?
7. Who plays Jim Halpert?
8. Which producer and writer of the show also appears as cousin Mose?
9. Who cameos as DeAngelo Vickers?
10. Who plays Todd Packer?
11. Who plays Andy Bernard?
12. Who plays Nellie Bertram?
13. Who appears as Charles Miner?
14. Who plays Kelly Kapoor?
15. Who plays Ryan Howard?

Answers on page 83

Season Eight

1. Who is the new CEO of Dunder Mifflin-Sabre?
2. Why do six warehouse workers all quit at the same time?
3. What is the name of the band formed by Andy, Darryl and Kevin?
4. Where does Andy take the office for a morale-boosting field trip?
5. Who does Dwight believe Darryl wants to look good for?
6. What is the name of the porcupine Dwight plants on his own desk in an attempt to frame Jim for pranking?
7. What is the quiz team name under which Kevin, Meredith, Erin and Kelly compete?
8. What does Andy (briefly) lose in Robert's pool?
9. Who tries to seduce Jim while they are working away in Tallahassee?
10. What medical issue does Dwight suffer in Tallahassee?
11. Who gets fired over the business plan for the Sabre store?
12. Who manages to replace Andy as Regional Manager?
13. What food does Darryl buy for he and Nellie?
14. What physical contest do Gabe and Dwight compete in against each other?
15. Who did David Wallace sell his "Suck It" concept to?

Answers on page 84

The Hardcore Nerd Round

1. Who is the only character to appear on-screen in every single episode of *The Office*?
2. Who delivers the last ever line on the show?
3. Which two cast members attended high school together?
4. What is the name of Jo Bennett's autobiography?
5. What is Todd Packer's car license plate?
6. Why does Andy refer to Jim as "Big Tuna"?
7. What had NBC originally planned on retitling the series as, in order to differentiate it from the British version?
8. Who was the first person to be cast in the show?
9. What is the name of the bar often visited by the staff?
10. What was Andy's birth name?
11. One of the dogs Andy adopts at the fundraiser also appears in another NBC series, where his character is named Champion. What is the series?
12. The of the four members of the *Anchorman* news team appear in *The Office*. Which one doesn't?
13. Which baseball player, who shares the same name as one of the characters, appears in the series?
14. What is Erin's real first name?
15. What is Gabe's middle name? Susan.

Answers on page 85

The UK Version

Are you a fan of the UK series of *The Office* too? Time to find out...

1. Which character is the UK equivalent of Michael?
2. Who is the UK version of Pam?
3. Who is the UK version of Dwight?
4. Who is the UK version of Jim?
5. Who is the UK version of Todd Packer?
6. Who is the UK version of Kevin?
7. Who is the UK version of Ryan?
8. Who is the UK version of Roy?
9. Who is the UK version of Jan?
10. What is the UK version of Dunder Mifflin?
11. When did the UK version first air?
12. How many seasons did the UK version run for?
13. And how many episodes did the UK series run for in total?
14. What is the theme tune to the UK version of *The Office*?
15. In which town is the UK version set?

Answers on page 86

Season Nine

1. What are the names of the twin new guys, nicknamed "The New Jim" and "Dwight Jr"?
2. What is the name of the cat Oscar adopts from Angela?
3. Which ex-bandmate claimed Andy's former nickname within his old a cappella group?
4. What instrument did Roy play at his wedding?
5. Who loses their anti-anxiety pill?
6. What language does Erin learn to impress Andy?
7. Which film does Pete know every line of?
8. Who deliberately gets a complaint to finish the feedback card stack?
9. Who shaves their head when the office is struck by lice?
10. What gets painted on Pam's mural?
11. Which former president does Pam say Jim looks like?
12. Who does Dwight hire back to the office as Quality Assurance Manager?
13. Who is the stripper at Angela's bachelorette party?
14. Who gets arrested in the finale?
15. Speaking of his past and present subordinates, who does Dwight say is his best friend?

Answers on page 87

Tiebreakers

Tied at the end of your quiz? Here's some "closest to" questions to help separate the wheat from the chaff.

1. How many episodes of *The Office* are there in total?
2. In which year did *The Office* first air?
3. And in which year did it finish?
4. According to Ryan's video for Dunder Mifflin Infinity, when was the company originally founded?
5. How many ageing dogs does Andy adopt at the silent auction fundraiser?
6. How much money does David Wallace donate to Robert California's "important new charity"?
7. How much does Ryan tell Pam she'll get back from her $50 investment after a year, as the result of his friend's college basketball algorithm?
8. What does Dwight claim was his birth weight?
9. In season one, a sign shows the Scranton office to be based on Slough Avenue (a reference to the setting of the original UK series). But what is the building number it is shown to have?
10. In season three, Jan gives Michael the biggest raise possible. What is the maximum percentage increase she is able to offer him?

11. To the nearest squared acre, how large is the surface area of Schrute Farms?

12. How many Primetime Emmys did *The Office* win? Three – Outstanding Comedy Series, Outstanding Writing for a Comedy Series (Greg Daniels) and Outstanding Directing for a Comedy Series (Jeffery Blitz).

13. How many hot dogs did Michael ask Pam to prepare for the staff eating competition to win his job?

14. According to David Wallace, how much did the CPR dummy ruined by Dwight cost?

15. How many years had Michael been working on *Threat Level Midnight* at the point he screened it to the office?

Answers on page 88

ANSWERS

Answers: Season One

1. 12 years.
2. Hillary Rodham Clinton.
3. Mixed berry.
4. Post-It notes.
5. His stapler.
6. Mr. Brown. Although unfortunately Michael sees this as a test.
7. "Martin Luther King Jr".
8. Angela.
9. "Absolutely, I do".
10. $25.
11. Meredith's.
12. Stanley.
13. They would work the following Saturday.
14. Katy.
15. Purses. Of which Dwight buys one, with a little influence from Jim.

Answers: Michael

1. "World's Best Boss".
2. God.
3. He invested it in a pyramid scheme.
4. Gary.
5. Five years old.
6. "Two-fifteenths".
7. 100, so that he could have 100 friends.
8. Bacon.
9. Pittsburgh Pirates.
10. (The) Michael Scott Paper Company.
11. 9,986,000.
12. Dennis the Menace.
13. 28 years.
14. Hottest in the Office.
15. His blue jeans.

Answers: That's What She Said

1. Gullet.
2. Rise.
3. Butter.
4. Smiling.
5. Toolbar.
6. Nook.
7. Thing.
8. Entice.
9. Post.
10. Queen.
11. Tickle.
12. Squeaks.
13. Came.
14. Magic.
15. Chest.

Answers: Dwight

1. Kurt.
2. A snake and a mongoose.
3. The chandelier from Tiffany's.
4. $80,000 a year.
5. The Crow.
6. Walking pneumonia.
7. Slayer. Unfortunately Clark was busy that night, ten months in the future.
8. His own circumcision.
9. Dwight Schrute's Gym for Muscles.
10. Mose.
11. His urologist.
12. Count Chocula.
13. 40.
14. A beet farm.
15. Forgetting to save the excess oil from a can of tuna.

Answers: Season Two

1. "Whitest Sneakers".
2. *Games of the First Dunder Mifflin Olympiad.*
3. Ryan. I defy you to not be singing Dwight's song in your own head at this point.
4. Devon. Who retaliates by smashing a pumpkin on Michael's car.
5. Chili's.
6. A $400 video iPod.
7. Captain Jack.
8. Learning to ice-skate.
9. Todd Packer.
10. Jim's.
11. The promise of the "best sex of [her] life".
12. Salesman of the Year.
13. "LittleKidLover".
14. Alicia Keys.
15. "Fart".

Answers: Jim

1. Big Tuna.
2. Duncan.
3. Australia.
4. Pete and Tom.
5. Philadelphia.
6. Outside a gas station.
7. One week.
8. Athlead.
9. Cece (Cecilia).
10. A teapot.
11. Future Dwight.
12. A computer chime.
13. Justin "Justice Beaver" Bieber.
14. Austin.
15. President of New Acquisitions.

Answers: Anagrams

1. Horny Award = Ryan Howard.
2. Battered Corn = Creed Bratton.
3. A Laborer Friction = Robert California.
4. Sitcom Chalet = Michael Scott.
5. Old Unloving Jeans = Jan Levinson-Gould.
6. Blind Lip Harry = Darryl Philbin.
7. Maybe Slep = Pam Beesly.
8. A Cavilled Wad = David Wallace.
9. Twitched Shrug = Dwight Schrute.
10. Hamper Jilt = Jim Halpert.
11. Wise Bagel = Gabe Lewis.
12. Lake Look Pry = Kelly Kapoor.
13. A Nerdy Brand = Andy Bernard.
14. Ennobled Frosty = Toby Flenderson.
15. Annoys Hustled = Stanley Hudson.

Answers: Pam

1. Three years.
2. Morgan.
3. Chili's, for sneaking drinks.
4. FreeCell.
5. Volleyball.
6. *On The Wings Of Love.*
7. Salesperson.
8. Phillip.
9. At the airport.
10. Yoghurt lids.
11. Graphic design.
12. *The Adventures of Jimmy Halpert.*
13. Charlie Chaplin. Unfortunately she has to keep the hat on, otherwise she looks like Hitler.
14. Helene.
15. Niagara Falls (and technically on a boat there).

Answers: Season Three

1. Stamford.
2. Angela.
3. *Call Of Duty*.
4. One year.
5. Ed Truck, who dies after being decapitated while drink-driving.
6. A pretzel.
7. Carol.
8. "Name repetition, personality mirroring and never breaking off a handshake."
9. Apollo Creed.
10. Benihana. Michael has to mark his date's arm with a Sharpie to be able to tell her apart from Andy's.
11. Pam.
12. Staples.
13. A bat.
14. "The jet skis". We're led to believe Kenny sold them for a loss earlier in the episode, and then Roy's antics mean that all of the money is handed over to compensate the bar owner.
15. Stanley's.

Answers: Pranks

1. Pencils.
2. Toby.
3. Hong Kong.
4. Mussolini.
5. $11.
6. "Diapers".
7. A metal detector.
8. Benjamin Franklin.
9. A tuxedo.
10. Morse code. They hired a nanny to allow them to do it. That's commitment.
11. An art contest. Poor Pam.
12. James Trickington.
13. Flowers for Pam.
14. Meatballs.
15. Steve.

Answers: Toby

1. Sasha.
2. Human Resources Representative, Scranton.
3. A duck.
4. Costa Rica.
5. Zip-lining.
6. His daughter's play. (Although he offers to miss the play because "what they do is not art".)
7. A rock.
8. "Suck on this!"
9. His own watch.
10. Poker (specifically Texas Hold'em).
11. Hardboiled detective/mystery novels.
12. The Scranton Strangler.
13. Social work.
14. Nellie.
15. Mushrooms.

Answers: Andy

1. Cornell.
2. Here Comes Treble.
3. Baines.
4. His nipples.
5. *Rainbow Connection*.
6. Sweeney Todd.
7. The Bahamas.
8. He punches through a wall.
9. He defecates on it.
10. *I Will Remember You*, by Sarah McLachlan.
11. On his butt.
12. *America's Next Great A Capella Star*.
13. "Baby Wawa".
14. Michelle Obama.
15. Admissions counsellor.

Answers: Season Four

1. Toby.
2. Meredith.
3. Sprinkles.
4. Dwight.
5. America, Irrigation, and Night-time.
6. *Harry Potter and the Goblet of Fire.*
7. Telemarketing.
8. Dwight Shelford.
9. Jim Samtanko, a guitar-playing, Philadelphia-based sportswriter.
10. A knife and a roll of duct tape.
11. *American Pie.*
12. The social networking component was invaded by sexual predators.
13. Dwight (after convincing him to sell it for less, then buying it from him himself and immediately advertising it for sale for $3,000 more than he paid Andy).
14. A single white sheet of paper.
15. Holly Flax.

Answers: Diseases

1. Mad Cow Disease = True.
2. Spontaneous Dental Hydroplosion = True.
3. Executive Bloating = False.
4. Severe Hangover = False.
5. General Illness = False.
6. Flesh-Eating Bacteria = True.
7. Hot Dog Fingers = True.
8. Anal Fissures = True.
9. Missing Nipple = False.
10. Government Created Killer Nanorobot Infection = True.
11. Nakatomi Syndrome = False.
12. Inverted Penis = True.
13. Count Choculitis = True.
14. Belgian Arthritis = False.
15. Excessively Small Thumbs = False.

Answers: Phyllis

1. Michael.
2. Karen.
3. Lapin.
4. Bob Vance (Vance Refrigeration).
5. Busiest Beaver. (Although the trophy reads "Bushiest Beaver".)
6. Easy Rider.
7. $1,000, to her husband Bob.
8. Morocco.
9. Dwight.
10. Pam.
11. It was the only way she could think of to get him to give her 6 weeks off for her honeymoon.
12. Toby's date.
13. Supreme Court Justice Sonia Sotomayor.
14. A pair of mittens (that can't get wet, cannot be dry cleaned, have to be hand-washed without water, wrung dry gently, and dried with a hair dryer on cool).
15. 42. And it lasted until she was 44.

Answers: The Accounting Department

1. Malone.
2. State Senator, Robert Lipton.
3. Scrantonicity.
4. Five.
5. Being a member of the Finer Things Club.
6. Kevin's Famous Chili.
7. "Keleven".
8. *Will & Grace*.
9. A poster of babies playing musical instruments.
10. A new copier.
11. He runs for state senator.
12. Phillip.
13. Oscar.
14. Kool Aid Man.
15. Monkey.

Answers: Season Five

1. A tapeworm. (Though Creed privately admits "It wasn't a tapeworm".)
2. Boner Champ.
3. *Physical*, by Olivia Newton John.
4 Astrid.
5. "Crime Reduces Innocence, Makes Everyone Angry I Declare".
6. The Joker.
7. Nashua.
8. Schrute Farms.
9. Caprese salad.
10. Buy new chairs.
11. Princess Unicorn.
12. Hilary Swank.
13. Kevin and Stanley, to the bemusement of them and everyone else.
14. Urine. It was urine.
15. "Two able-bodied men."

Answers: Dwight's Perfect Crime

1. Tiffany's.
2. Chandelier.
3. Tiffany.
4. Uniforms.
5. Mexico.
6. Canada.
7. Cold.
8. Thirty
9. Chief of police.
10. Paris.
11. Trocadero.
12. Berlin.

Answers: Kelly & Ryan

1. Kapoor.
2. A *Twilight* poster.
3. *Exposure in the Workplace*.
4. The University of Scranton's Kania School of Management.
5. Jennifer Lopez.
6. Dunder Mifflin Infinity.
7. Darryl.
8. Fraud, after double-counting office sales as website sales to artificially increase the firm's figures.
9. *America's Got Talent*.
10. A bowling alley.
11. WUPHF.
12. Ravi.
13. Ohio, which is home to Miami University for Ravi. Unfortunately Kelly thought she was moving to Florida.
14. Drake.
15. Strawberries.

Answers: Season Six

1. Poop-ball.
2. Jim.
3. *Forever*, by Chris Brown.
4. Jim.
5. He snips his tie in half.
6. Puerto Rico.
7. Kevin.
8. Koi.
9. *Belles, Bourbon, and Bullets.*
10. Jim, framed by Dwight to make it appear as though he picked himself.
11. A nutcracker. (Though Dwight initially believes it is a gun.)
12. "Suck It", a vacuum designed to collect children's toys.
13. Cookie Monster.
14. Kelly.
15. Dwight.

Answers: Stanley

1. Teri.
2. Cynthia.
3. Three sugars and five creams.
4. Crosswords.
5. A wood carving he made of her as a bird.
6. Melissa.
7. "Shove it up your butt!"
8. "Fine Work".
9. Seven.
10. A toaster.
11. He is the narrator.
12. Utica.
13. Pretzel Day.
14. Dwight's fake fire.
15. Phyllis.

Answers: Who Said It?

1. Kelly.
2. Stanley.
3. Michael.
4. Kevin.
5. Andy.
6. Phyllis.
7. Angela.
8. Dwight.
9. Toby.
10. Darryl.
11. Jim.
12. Todd Packer.
13. Kevin.
14. Meredith.
15. Pam.

Answers: Season Seven

1. Luke.
2. Steamtown Mall. In fairness they only wouldn't serve him because his hands were covered in beet juice, so they assumed he'd killed someone.
3. It's hiding a cold sore on his lip.
4. Popeye, Olive Oyl and Swee'Pea.
5. Arcade Fire.
6. *Glee*.
7. Washington University Public Health Fund.
8. Fear.
9. Darryl.
10. "Three years' salary".
11. Best Dundies Host.
12. *The King's Speech*.
13. Colorado.
14. *Bring Me To Life*, by Evanescence.
15. Slam-dunking a basketball.

Answers: Complete the Quote

1. "Afraid of how much they love me".
2. "Kleenex".
3. "PowerPoints".
4. "Chair".
5. "BANKRUPTCY".
6. "A little stitious".
7. "Dog food".
8. "Helen Mirren".
9. "Bacon".
10. "Dementors".
11. "Dot dot dot, dot dot".
12. "Sparrow".
13. "*National Treasure.*"
14. "Fire".
15. "Horse Flyer".

Answers: Cast & Crew

1. Ricky Gervais and Stephen Merchant.
2. Greg Daniels.
3. Steve Carell.
4. Rainn Wilson.
5. Randall Einhorn.
6. Jenna Fischer.
7. John Krasinski.
8. Michael Schur.
9. Will Ferrell.
10. David Koechner.
11. Ed Helms.
12. Catherine Tate.
13. Idris Elba.
14. Mindy Kaling.
15. B. J. Novak.

Answers: Season Eight

1. Robert California.
2. They win $950,000 on the lottery.
3. Kevin and the Zits.
4. Gettysburg.
5. Val Kilmer.
6. Henrietta.
7. The Einsteins.
8. The engagement ring with which he intends to propose to Jessica.
9. Cathy.
10. Appendicitis.
11. Todd Packer.
12. Nellie.
13. Tacos.
14. A thigh curl contest. Sadly Jim takes and subsequently doctors a photo to make the pair look like they're having a girly sleepover.
15. The US military.

Answers: The Hardcore Nerd Round

1. Dwight.
2. Pam - "There's a lot of beauty in ordinary things. Isn't that kind of the point?"
3. John Krasinski and B. J. Novak. They were also on a little league baseball team together. Small world.
4. *Take A Good Look*.
5. "WLHUNG".
6. Because on the day they met, Jim ate a tuna sandwich for lunch.
7. *An American Workplace*.
8. B. J. Novak.
9. Poor Richard's.
10. Walter (or Walter Baines Bernard Jr to be precise).
11. *Parks and Recreation*. I like to imagine Champion plays the same character in both series.
12. Paul Rudd.
13. Ryan Howard. (He has the same name as Ryan Howard.)
14. Kelly. Charles Miner decides it would be too confusing to have two Kellys in the office, so she uses her middle name.
15. Susan.

Answers: The UK Version

1. David Brent.
2. Dawn Tinsley.
3. Gareth Keenan.
4. Tim Canterbury.
5. Chris "Finchy" Finch. (The writers also made Packer's middle name Finch.)
6. Keith Bishop.
7. Ricky Howard.
8. Lee. (We never learn his surname.)
9. Jennifer Taylor-Clarke.
10. Wernham Hogg.
11. 2001.
12. Two, plus a Christmas special.
13. Fourteen.
14. *Handbags and Gladrags*, by Rod Stewart.
15. Slough.

Answers: Season Nine

1. Pete Miller and Clark Green.
2. Comstock. AKA the senator's favorite cat.
3. Broccoli Rob.
4. Piano.
5. Nellie.
6. Dothraki.
7. *Die Hard*.
8. Pam.
9. Meredith.
10. Butts.
11. Nixon.
12. Devon.
13. Meredith's son, Jake.
14. Creed.
15. Pam.

Answers: Tiebreakers

1. 201.
2. 2005.
3. 2013.
4. 1949.
5. 12.
6. One million dollars.
7. $5,000.
8. 13 lbs, 5 oz.
9. 1725 Slough Avenue.
10. 12%.
11. 60 square acres.
12. Three – Outstanding Comedy Series, Outstanding Writing for a Comedy Series (Greg Daniels) and Outstanding Directing for a Comedy Series (Jeffery Blitz).
13. 800.
14. $3,500.
15. 11 years.

Thanks for reading, quizzer! If you've enjoyed the book, please leave a review on Amazon: it only takes a minute and it really helps! Take care.

- Alex.

OTHER BOOKS BY ALEX MITCHELL

Quizzin' Nine-Nine: A Brooklyn Nine-Nine Quiz Book
Parks & Interrogation: A Parks & Recreation Quiz Book
Q & AC-12: A Line of Duty Quiz Book
Know Your Schitt: A Schitt's Creek Quiz Book
Examilton: A Hamilton Quiz Book
Stranger Thinks: A Stranger things Quiz Book
The El Clued Brothers: A Peep Show Quiz Book

Printed in Great Britain
by Amazon